Portrait of Cats

Portrait of Cats
Angela Sayer

Hamlyn
London · New York · Sydney · Toronto

Acknowledgements

Special acknowledgement is made to Anne Cumbers who contributed the majority of the illustrations in the book. Other contributors were: Animal Graphics, Barnaby's Picture Library, Camera Press, Fox Photos, Will Green, Pictorial Press, Syndication International, Nicholas Wright, Tony Stone Associates, Spectrum Colour Library and Pictor/Zefa.

Published by
The Hamlyn Publishing Group Limited
London . New York . Sydney . Toronto
Astronaut House, Feltham, Middlesex, England
Copyright © The Hamlyn Publishing Group Limited 1975
ISBN 0 600 37105 0

Printed in Hong Kong

Contents

Introduction

To the uninitiated, a cat is just a cat, and even the genuine cat-lover may receive something of a shock in discovering just how many different cat breeds are officially recognized throughout the world.

Pedigree cats are divided into two basic types, defined by their bone structure and general conformation. The first type is short and stocky; powerful in appearance; with short legs, back, neck and tail; tiny ears; and big, round eyes set in a large, full-cheeked head. The second type is lighter in bone structure; lithe and slender; with long legs, back, neck and tail; a longer head; large, pricked ears; and oriental or almond-shaped eyes.

The first group can be further classified according to hair length. Those cats with long, flowing coats are known as the Persian or longhaired breeds, and those with short, close coats as British shorthaired, American shorthaired or European shorthaired, depending upon the country in which the variety originated or was developed.

The second group is divided also, for although these svelte cats are only bred in shorthaired varieties, the group includes the very popular Siamese which, in this book, will be treated in a separate section. The other varieties within this group are known collectively as the foreign shorthaired and include exotic, self-coloured cats derived from Siamese ancestors, as well as the older, well-established breeds such as the Abyssinian, Russian Blue and Burmese, and the uniquely curled rex.

Two fairly rare breeds of cat, meticulously bred for purity and never outcrossed with any other breeds, are the Birman and the Turkish. This has ensured that their unique features and intermediate type have been maintained through the generations, so that they do not really fit into any of the main groups of breeds, but require a special section of their own which we shall call the semi-longhaired group.

Several unusual varieties of cat are bred and fully recognized in America for breeding and show purposes, which are not known in Britain, and range from the selectively developed Peke-face Persian to the hairless mutant, the Sphynx. These interesting varieties have also been given their own section.

Finally, we have perhaps the most special cats of all, those which do not fit into any 'type' or 'standard of points of perfection', the common or garden house-cat. No genuine cat book is complete without a section on non-pedigree cats, for every true cat-lover will maintain that there is no such thing as an 'ordinary' cat. Even the most famed of breeding catteries have their mongrel pets, receiving exactly the same food, attention and love as the potential prize-winners.

In Britain, the Governing Council of the Cat Fancy looks after the interests of all matters pertaining to the breeding, exhibiting and registration of pedigree cats. It also has specialist committees which deal with aspects of cat care, genetics and cat genealogy, and approve standards of points for new breeds, grant breed numbers and championship status. It issues stud lists and stud books and presents champion challenge certificates at appropriate shows. The Council is composed of delegates elected annually by the members of affiliated cat clubs, societies and associations, and is run on very democratic lines. Most other countries with large pedigree cat populations have governing bodies very similar to that of Britain.

To become a member of the Cat Fancy, one has merely to be a registered owner of a pedigree cat or kitten,

or to become a fully paid-up member of any affiliated cat club, and entrance to the Fancy can be the curtain-up to a very exciting and fulfilling hobby. Cat shows are held all through the year in Britain, at least one and sometimes two or three championship shows being held per month, and these are spread over the length and breadth of the country from Montrose to Newton Abbot. In America, many more shows are held, and as there are several registering bodies, each may be run on slightly different lines. It is possible at an American show for a cat to become a full champion in one day, whereas, in Britain, even a top cat will need a minimum of three cat shows to achieve this status.

As there are so many varieties of cat available, it is important for the would-be cat owner to choose carefully so that he is sure of selecting the breed best suited to his home, taste and temperament, and it is hoped that the beautiful illustrations in this book will help anyone who is in a state of indecision. Healthy kittens, kept free of accidents, will grow up and live for a very long while, so it is advisable to spend time in thought initially, so that the cat that will adorn the hearth for so long is the right cat.

Having read about the breeds and perused the pictures, perhaps a visit to a local cat show to see the variety in the flesh should be the next step, or the local veterinary surgeon might know of a breeder of repute within easy reach. Otherwise, many newspapers and periodicals carry cat advertisements, and a visit to see the kittens can be arranged without any obligation to buy. Non-pedigreed kittens are usually readily available from farms and pet shops, but all kittens, whether pedigree or not, require the same attention and food, and should be vaccinated against feline infectious enteritis immediately.

Breeding pedigreed cats is a pleasant hobby if one has the time, patience and space for rearing kittens. It is usual to start with a female kitten which has been recommended by the breeder as suitable for use as a future brood queen. At maturity, the young female will come into heat and is then taken to a previously booked stud male for service. It is usual to leave the queen with the stud owner for two or three days so that she may settle and mating can take place, then the fee is paid and she is brought quietly home. If all has gone well, her litter should be born some sixty-five days later, with the minimum of fuss, and the joy of rearing the little family can be shared between the proud little mother and her owner. At six weeks, the kittens start weaning themselves and are fully independent at ten weeks. They should be kept another two or three weeks, however, and wormed and vaccinated before going to their new homes.

Cats that are not to be bred from, whether pedigree or not, should be neutered by a veterinary surgeon at about four to six months of age. Whether the kitten is male or female, the operation is very routine and has no unpleasant side effects. If left entire, males will eventually fight, wander, and spray the house with extremely strong-smelling urine, while females will have continuous periods of oestrus if confined, and very regular mongrel litters of kittens if allowed to wander.

Whatever your interests in cats may be, they are certain to be enhanced as you turn the pages of this book, and you are sure of finding the cat of your dreams in *Portrait of Cats*.

Longhaireds

It is thought that the first domesticated cats in the British Isles were introduced by the invading Roman armies, and it is certain that all these creatures, much prized for their ability to keep down vermin in the corn stores, were shortcoated. Only later, in the sixteenth century, were the first longcoated cats brought to Britain, having travelled first from Ankara in Turkey and Iran, then known as Angora and Persia, to France. They were greatly admired for the beauty of their coats, and carried across the English Channel to become prized possessions in the homes of noblemen.

These longcoated cats were known as Angora and Persian cats respectively, and were rare and thus very valuable. The Angoras were mainly white in colour and their fur was extremely silky and inclined to fall straight down from the spine, while the Persians were generally black or slate-blue with a firmer texture to the coat. Other differences were also apparent in bone structure, the Angoras being, on the whole, slighter in build, with a more pointed face and larger ears. Interbreeding between the two varieties was carried out through the centuries and the Persian type gradually superseded that of the Angora.

At the turn of the twentieth century, interest in the planned breeding of cats had begun and the first cat shows were held in Britain and in America. The owners of unusual cats began to keep records, and the first pedigrees came into being. Groups of people interested in the same types of cat formed clubs and societies, and thus the Cat Fancy began.

In the longhaired breeds, each colour variety has its own set standard of points of perfection – that is to say, there is a set list of desired features, each feature being allotted a number of points, and the whole adding up to 100 points for a perfect specimen. For example, the Blue Persian of today, the most popular of all the longhaired varieties, has the following scale of points: coat, twenty; condition, ten; head, twenty-five; eyes, twenty; body, fifteen; tail, ten. The standard of points for each variety is worked out by the breed's society, and points are allocated in accordance with the feature needing emphasis. In the Blue Persian, above, it may be seen that the most outstanding feature is the head, for which twenty-five points are given, and the coat and eyes are also highly rated. In Black Persians the density of coat colour is considered more important, and so in this variety the coat is given twenty-five points and the head, twenty.

Despite the slight deviations in the points structure, the general standard for all longhaired cats is the same and calls for a very broad, round head, with tiny, tufted ears set well apart; full, round cheeks; a short, broad nose; and very large, round eyes. Obviously, the coat is of utmost importance, and should be very dense, soft and silky, and never have a woolly, or harsh texture. The short, stocky body is supported by low-hocked, sturdy legs, and the tail, known as the 'brush', must be very short and full, and must never have any sign of a thickened vertebra or kink. The long, soft fur around the head is known as the 'ruff' and for show purposes is brushed up to form an elegant frame for the face.

Obviously, very few cats have all these attributes, for the standard of perfection is the breeders' ideal cat. Many cats come very near to achieving the standard, however, and on maturity, these specimens quickly reach full championship status, and are greatly admired by the cat-show public. Longhaired kittens can be shown from the age of two months in Britain and are considered to be adult at nine months, when they may start to compete for their championship. In America, however, kittens may not start their show career until they reach four months of age, but are considered to be adult at eight months.

Many of the longhaired varieties are known by their coat colour in the title of their breed – for instance, a plain black, longhaired cat is known simply as the Black Longhair or Black Persian. Cats with fur of only one colour throughout are known collectively as the self-colours; those with classically blotched markings are called tabby; and those with particolours have their own titles. For example, the selfs include Black, White, Blue, Cream and Red Persians, and the Whites can be either Orange-eyed, Blue-eyed or Odd-eyed. There are Brown, Red and Silver Tabbies, and the unusual Smoke Persians in Black or Blue, with each hair shading down to the pure-white undercoat. The particolours can be Blue-cream, Tortoiseshell, Tortoiseshell and White, or Bi-coloured. The Chinchilla is perhaps the most photogenic of all the longhaired cats, and its sparkling appearance is caused by the elusive silver gene, each white hair being lightly tipped with black. The nose leather and incredible emerald or aquamarine eyes are also outlined with black, the whole presenting a most exotic and pleasing appearance.

The introduction of the Himalayan genetic factor into Persian cat breeding programmes has been carefully carried out in recent years by a few dedicated breeders, and has resulted in the production of the Colourpoint Persian, known in America as the Himalayan cat. This is a cat of full Persian characteristics, but with the distinctive coat pattern and coloration of the Siamese, complete with blue eye-colour.

Persian cats are delightful to own, and each variety has minor traits which make it the perfect pet for some household. They do, however, need daily grooming in order to keep the long, flowing coat free from troublesome mats of hair, and it is essential that anyone contemplating the purchase of a Persian kitten should be prepared to undertake this regular brushing and combing. For showing, it is often necessary to bath a Persian, especially the lighter breeds, so that the cat is shown with its coat in perfect order. Therefore, in choosing a show specimen, it is imperative that full consideration is given to temperament, as well as to health and beauty.

Black Persian kittens often have rusty-looking or shaded coats, but these specimens sometimes grow up to be the densest Blacks of all. Therefore, kittens selected for exhibition purposes have to picked on type and conformation alone.

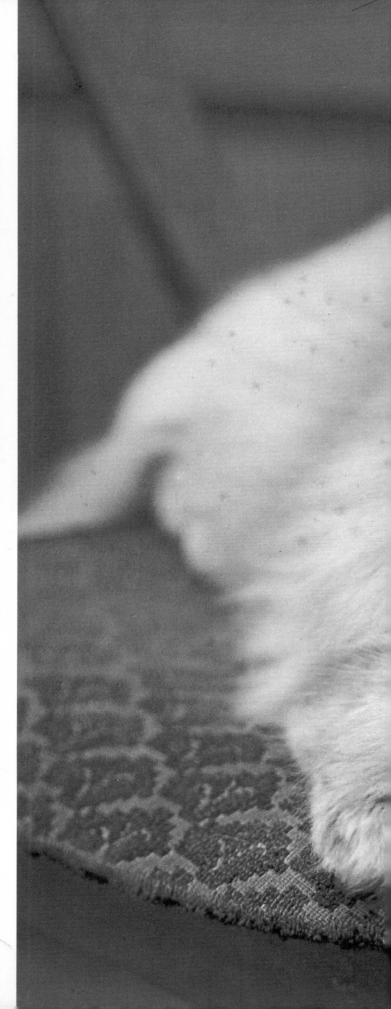

Above
These seven-week-old Blue Longhaired kittens are too young to compete in cats shows anywhere in the world, for strict rules are laid down as regards minimum age requirements and were formulated for the protection and general welfare of young show cats.

Right
Blue-cream Persians are always female, due to the sex-linked effect of the red gene responsible, in dilute form, for their coloration. In America, the two pastel colours of the coat must be boldly patched for a good show specimen, while in Britain, a softly intermingled effect is preferred.

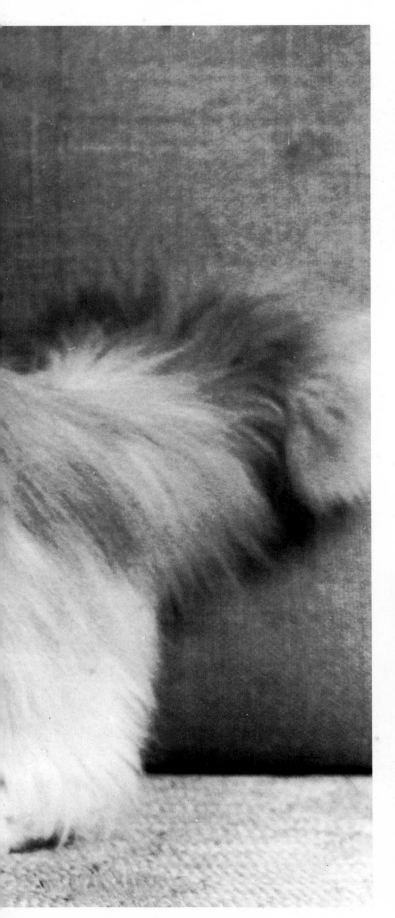

Left
Bicoloured Longhaireds may be bred in any usual cat colour plus white. The markings must be as symmetrically arranged as possible, giving the even and balanced look seen in this wonderful example, where the two halves of the face appear to be mirror images.

Above
The Red Self Longhair is known in America as the Solid Red or Red Persian, but is rare on both sides of the Atlantic, for this is one of the most difficult of all breeds to produce to perfection, and outcrossing to other Persian colours necessitates long-term breeding programmes.

Below
The Orange-eyed White Persian is known as the Copper-eyed in America and was first recorded officially in 1889. However, separate breed classes were not given for the variety in Britain until the late 1930s, since when many top show awards have been taken by the breed.

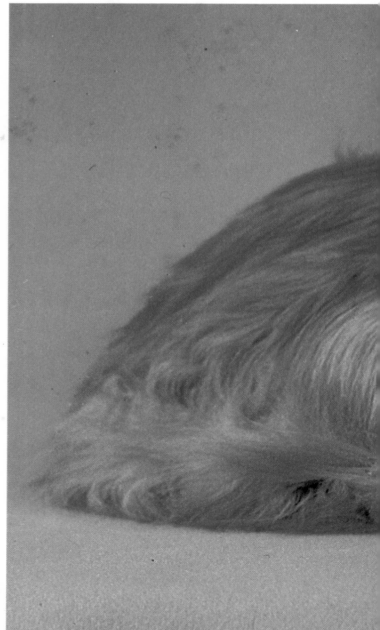

Far left

This Blue Colourpoint is a magnificent example of the
results of careful selective breeding. In this cat, the true
Persian type can be seen: the short nose and very firm
chin; round, full face; compact body; and sturdy
legs – all hallmarks of an excellent longhair.

Left

Most Persian kittens get into all sorts of mischief and
are great climbers. Like all young cats, these Creams
like to find boxes or other confined areas and the added
attraction of the titbits on the bird table proved
irresistible.

Below

Originally, the Longhaired Red Tabby cats were known
as the Oranges, a very apt name. Today, however, the
standard calls for the coat to be a deep, rich red with
darker markings clearly defined and continued down
the chest, legs and tail.

Above
Blue Persians may be of any blue shade, although the lighter tones seem to be preferred, if sound to the roots. The fur is soft, silky and very thick, forming a wonderful ruff around the head, and the deep-orange or copper eyes are most expressive.

Right
Noted for his intelligence and strength of character, the Blue Persian loves to be the centre of attraction and makes the perfect house pet, adoring his owner and remaining kittenish to the end of his days, the life span of a neuter averaging about fifteen years.

Below

In this picture we can see one of the oldest established breeds, the Cream Persian, accompanied by one which has only recently achieved full championship status, the Cream and White Bicolour. The superb cat shown here has the desired even and well-distributed areas of colour, on white.

Below right

All kittens are irresistible, but this Blue Persian is particularly appealing, and is of excellent show type. His coat is very sound throughout, unusual in one so young, and his eye-colour promises to be of the desired deep-orange or copper shade.

Left
The best Silver Tabby Longhairs are born black, except for the legs and flanks, and the silver ground-colour slowly develops from the legs upwards, until the true markings appear around the age of six months. Type is less extreme than in the self-coloured Persians.

Below
The pedigree Brown Tabby Longhair is quite different from the semi-longcoated tabbies seen on farms, for the exhibition variety has a coat of a striking sable shade and the classic, marbled pattern is traced in dense black, with striking black pencilling on the head.

Right
Despite his rather glowering expression, the Smoke has a most even temperament and is often to be seen competing for the supreme honours at cat shows. When in full coat, the silver undercoat is easily visible, contrasting strikingly with the dark topcoat.

Below right
Contrary to common belief, Red Tabby Persians may be either male or female, and the females are not worth vast sums, although, as in any breed, a good specimen is valuable for breeding purposes. This prizewinning male shows the classic 'M' mark on his forehead.

Often called the 'cat of contrasts', the silver ruff of this Smoke frames his black face and highlights the orange eye-colour. The effect is caused by the thick white undercoat overlaid by a black topcoat, affording a shot-silk effect.

This Chinchilla kitten of six months does not show the
black tipping which will make her sparkle as an adult,
but already she poses prettily, her exquisite emerald eyes
outlined in black, and her full coat forming the perfect
frame for her face.

Above
Appearing to bow to his public, this young Chinchilla male is of outstanding promise. The thick coats of this variety and their resistance to illness enable them to be raised easily in outdoor catteries. Despite their exotic appearance, they need the minimum of care.

Right
Although wholly Persian in looks and nature, the Colourpoint has a mind of her own if aroused, and this direct look is a warning not to take any liberties. Large and expressive eyes have been one of the features desired by Colourpoint breeders which has been difficult to achieve.

Left
Tiny ears and a broad, full-cheeked head are typical of the Longhaired Cream, and in a good, pale-coated specimen, carefully prepared for exhibition purposes, will help to ensure top honours at the cat show.

Below
The soft, flowing coat of the Longhaired Cream must be pure and sound throughout, and palest cream in colour, which offsets the large, deep-copper eyes to perfection. The standard of points penalizes this breed for tabby markings or traces of red in the coat.

Right

In great demand as models for stage, screen and television, the Chinchilla makes a perfect star! This female is representative of the breed which has been voted 'most beautiful cat', her calm, though alert expression indicating an even temperament, so essential for the working cat.

Below

Called the Calico Cat by the American Fancy, the Longhaired Tortoiseshell and White is another variety in which males very rarely occur. Very strikingly patched with red, black and white, the eye-colour for this variety should be orange or copper.

Smoke Persian kittens undergo many changes in appearance from birth, and only experienced breeders can pick a future champion until about the age of six or seven months. However, the bone structure and head type can be assessed even at the tender age of four weeks, as in this promising youngster.

Right
The Colourpoint Persian, known as the Himalayan in America, became officially recognized in Britain in 1955 after some eight years of careful breeding by a small group of enthusiasts, in which the Siamese factor for restricting the colour to the 'points' was introduced into a Persian strain.

Above
Among the most recent of recognized varieties, the Red Colourpoint Persian is almost correct for type and conformation, although breeders have found difficulty in reducing the noselength and the size of the ears. This kitten has excellent points and eye-colour.

Right
The exhibition Longhaired Silver Tabby is always a show-stopper, for this breed is rarely seen on the bench nowadays, possibly because perfect specimens are so difficult to breed. The classic tabby pattern is etched in black on a silver ground, and the eyes may be green or hazel.

British shorthaireds

The name 'British' was given to shorthaired, squarely built cats to distinguish them from those of supposedly foreign origins. The British shorthaireds are built on the same lines as their longhaired cousins, the Persians, while the foreign cats are their complete antithesis. Colour variation and coat patterns in the British are also very similar to those of the Persians. Similar varieties, known as American or domestic shorthaireds, are found in America and these have almost identical standards of points.

Points of perfection in the British shorthaireds emphasize the full-chested, sturdy body; short, well-proportioned legs; powerful neck; and short, thick-based tail. The head must be well-rounded, with full, well-developed cheeks and topped with tiny, wide-spaced ears. The eyes must be wide-open, large and round, and the nose, although short, should not be as flattened as that of the longhaired cats. Manx cats are also classed as British, but are unique in being without tails. They also have a slightly different, double-textured coat, and have very long hind legs, possibly to compensate in balancing when climbing, a function usually performed by the tail in other breeds.

British shorthaireds are known by their coloration, such as Black, White, Blue, Cream and Red in the self-colours, and the British White can also be Orange-eyed, Blue-eyed or Odd-eyed. In addition to the Brown, Red and Silver Tabbies, as found in the Persian breeds, British tabby markings can be modified to clearly defined spotting, and these cats may be of any colour, all being known as Spotted cats. The spotting in this variety is considered all important, and fifty per cent of the total show points are given for this characteristic.

Particoloured British shorthaireds also include the Blue-cream, Tortoiseshell, Tortoiseshell and White, and the Bicoloured. Tortoiseshell cats must have coats of black, dark red and light red patches, clear and well-defined, with no blurred or tabby markings, and, if possible, a red blaze to bisect the face between the orange, copper or hazel eyes. The Tortoiseshell and White has additional white areas, which must not predominate, and a good specimen will have all colours equally distributed over the whole of the head, tail and body, with a white blaze. Blue-cream cats are merely dilute tortoiseshells, but, strange as it may seem, in this variety the colours are required to be softly intermingled, and not patched, in England, although patches are preferred in America.

Spotted cats can be of any colour normally found in British shorthaireds, and the majority of show points is awarded for the clarity of the spotting rather than type, so this little red fisherman would score highly in a show.

Bicoloured cats are, as the name suggests, cats of two colours, but they must not have haphazard markings. The coloured areas must be clearly and evenly distributed, with not more than two-thirds of the coat being coloured and not more than one half being white. These cats may be bred in any colour plus white, and although only recently accepted officially for show and championship purposes by the Governing Council of the Cat Fancy, bicoloured black and white cats were shown in the early cat shows, when they were most popular, and known as Magpie cats.

British shorthaired cats are delightful to own, and very undemanding as pets. They can live happily within the framework of a normal family and get along well with most breeds of dog. They are excellent hunters, and clean in all their habits, but do not seem to do so well when completely confined to the house in contrast to their foreign cousins. Easy to groom, the British shorthaireds can be kept in show condition at all times by daily handgrooming – rubbing the coat with the fingers to remove dead hair, then smoothing back into place with firm, even strokes. Loose hairs can be combed out weekly, when the ears and claws can also receive any necessary attention. Before the show, a soiled cat can be prepared by giving a bran-bath. Some ordinary bran is heated on a tray in the oven, then placed in a large bowl. The cat has the hot bran rubbed well into the coat, left for a few minutes, then brushed out. This cleans and freshens the coat of all shorthaired varieties.

Breeding British shorthaireds can be very rewarding, if at times very frustrating, for the colours and patterns can be very elusive in some varieties. Generations of careful selection have gone into the perfection of form that we see on the show benches today. Much thought is given to the selection of the stud male, and it is important that his outstanding features should be those which are lacking or deficient in the queen. For instance, if the female Silver Tabby has outstanding markings but is a little too long in the nose, and large in the ears, the male chosen should have a superb head, even if his markings leave a little to be desired. With luck, one or two of the kittens may combine the best features of both sire and dam, and they are the ones that will be earmarked for future breeding plans.

Queens usually have fairly small litters compared to the foreign shorthairs. Three kittens seem to be the average, but these are sturdy and soon prove to be quite enough for the mother's lactational capabilities. Eyes open in the young ones at about seven to ten days, and weaning on to solids can begin at around four to five weeks, when the mother cat will encourage the kittens to use a toilet tray. British queens love to hunt for their kittens and if not allowed access to the garden, she should be provided with some 'prey' in the form of a long, thin strip of raw meat, which she may present to her offspring, flipping it around to excite their hunting instincts.

Far left
Of extremely good type, this Orange-eyed British White poses for the camera. Careful grooming is essential for all the whites, especially before a cat show, and regular dry-shampooing with special grooming powder prevents yellow staining.

Above
This picture shows how two varieties with separate breed numbers occur in the same litter, for the modified coat pattern is due merely to a slight variation in one gene. In the Spotted, the tabby pattern forms into clearly defined spots, and in the Tabby, the classic arrangement of whorls and rings can be seen.

Left
Unlike the non-pedigreed, shorthaired, black cat, the British Black has a soft, dense, black coat without a single white hair, and instead of the ordinary green eyes, those of the pedigreed black are a deep-orange, striking in the coal-black face.

Left
The rump of a good Manx is supposed to be as round as an orange with a small depression where the tail should be. This little mackerel-striped Manx kitten certainly seems to fulfil these requirements.

Below
Unique in the cat world is the completely tailless Manx cat, believed to have been introduced to the Isle of Man from a wrecked ship of the Spanish Armada in 1588. Manx may be bred in any normal cat colour with corresponding eye-colour.

Above
In the Mackerel Tabby, a modification of the pattern
apparent in the Spotted cat can be seen, for instead
of breaking into clear spots, the coloured bands run down
in unbroken lines from the spine of the cat, causing
a striped effect. Mackerel Tabbies can be shown, and
are given breed numbers according to their
corresponding Tabby cousins.

Above right
Shorthaired Bicolours may be of any colour plus white
and this handsome Blue and White is of really top British
type, with good width between the ears, a short nose
and full cheeks, and a short, close-coupled body. His
symmetrical facial markings are also very pleasing.

Right
Silver Tabby Shorthaired kittens are born very dark
with light feet and sides, and gradually lighten up until
the correct pattern may be seen etched all over the body.
Even at this interim stage in their development, these
young ones are most appealing.

Left
Called Magpie cats at the turn of the century, the Bicoloureds went out of fashion to be revived once more and given full status by the Governing Council of the Cat Fancy. The revised standard of 1971 enables any solid colour plus white, to be bred.

Above
White kittens are born with blue eyes, whether they are Orange-eyed, Blue-eyed or Odd-eyed White Shorthaireds, and the baby-blue colour changes at about nine to ten weeks to the adult shade. This Odd-eyed cat is probably the result of mating Orange-eyed with Blue-eyed, and unlike his Blue-eyed parent, he will have perfect hearing.

47

Top
Even in these new-born and still blind British Blue babies, the true shorthaired type can be seen in the roundness of the heads and the short and stocky little legs. The ghost tabby markings are apparent on many self-coloured kittens and disappear as the fur grows longer and closer.

Above
British Blue queens make excellent mothers, having firm, even litters of three or four sturdy kittens, without any fuss or bother. The kittens eyes open at seven to ten days and they stay in the nest box for about six weeks, when they start to wean themselves by tasting their mother's food.

This proud British Blue is looking every inch the Grand
Champion that he is, his gentle expression being typical
of his breed. He shows the desired full-cheeked face and
sturdy, cobby build called for in the standard of points.

Below
This British Cream kitten is full of promise as a future
show winner and stud cat. His light coat is virtually
free from ghost markings and he is well balanced and
firm.

Right
Shorthaired Creams are very difficult to breed to show
standard, as ghost tabby markings can appear from time
to time in even the soundest of short cream coats. As
can be seen in this kitten, type is very good, and this
is a most attractive variety to own.

Below

Silver Spotted cats are becoming increasingly popular and conform closely to the demanding standards laid down for them. Well-knit, cobby and muscular, the Spottie is an active, agile cat, with a pleasing nature.

Right

Few British Red Tabby cats are seen at cat shows, possibly because the correct type has been hard to achieve. Both the classic and mackerel tabby markings are permissible, but in either case the colour must be really dense and the pattern quite distinct from the ground colour, as seen in this young cat.

Below right

This excellent black and white Manx cat, or 'rumpie' has the characteristic stance due to the hind legs being comparatively longer than the forelegs. When seen in action, these cats tend to hop with the back legs kept close together, and this feature was noted, causing the breed to be known as 'bunny' cats in the past.

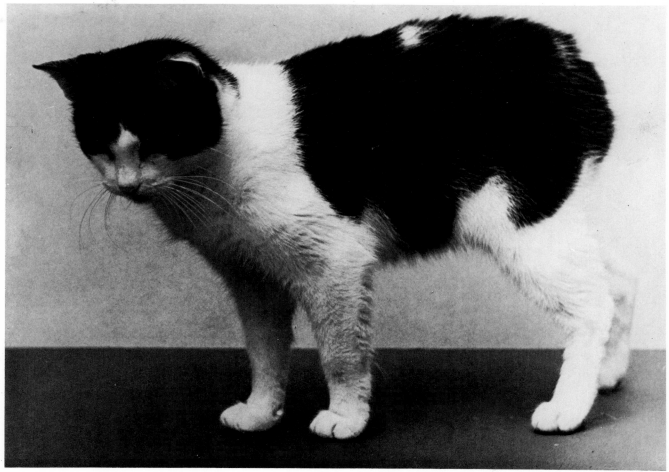

In the British Silver Tabby, the black marbling is very clearly defined against the silver background making this one of the most striking varieties in the British shorthaired section. Although often shown, and very popular, they are shy and gentle cats.

British Tabby cats may be had with mackerel markings, or with spots instead of the classic design, and the Spotted cats have a separate breed number. This pensive Silver Spotted kitten is perfectly marked, and looks like a little snow-leopard.

Above
Manx cats should be completely tailless, when they are known as 'rumpies', but kittens with tails of all lengths may be born to Manx parents, and those with a vestigial tail, like this beautiful white, are known as 'stumpies'.

Right
The massive head and overall build of this magnificent British Brown Tabby, coupled with the excellence of the marbled pattern, complete with 'oyster' marks, 'mayor's chains' and distinctive head markings, have made him virtually unbeatable at any cat show.

Far right
The red blaze bisecting the face of this striking Tortoiseshell and White Shorthair gives her a somewhat bizarre expression, and while a white blaze is preferable, according to the standard, the patching on this female is very attractive indeed.

56

Foreign shorthaireds

The foreign shorthaired cats are as different to the British shorthaireds as chalk is to cheese. With minor exceptions within the breeds, all foreigns must have long and slim bodies, legs and tails; small oval feet; and variously long, wedge-shaped heads with large, pricked ears and oriental eyes. They are medium in size, all short-coated, and each variety has a completely separate standard of points of perfection, plus its own distinctive personality.

Although some foreign breeds sport evocative foreign names, most have, in fact, been bred to their present forms in Britain and then exported all over the world. There are exceptions – for instance, the Burmese travelled the opposite way, for this cat was developed in America, and was then imported into Britain in 1947. Most breeds have some ties with the country of their title, but these are often difficult to substantiate, and are not really very important. It is the judicious inter-breeding and outcrossing by selective breeders in the past century that have given us all the delightful foreign shorthairs that we see today, and more are being added as successful applications for recognition of new varieties are made to the governing bodies each year.

That selective breeding principles have been successful over the years has been most apparent in the foreign shorthaired varieties, for in determining which cats should be used for developmental breeding programmes, discerning breeders have given much thought and care to the eradication of undesirable features. This has been shown up in the recent results, and the newer varieties are noticeably free from the defects so apparent in their ancestors – crossed eyes, kinked tails, cleft palates, projecting sterna, bone defects and faulty dentition are things of the past. The new generation of foreign cat has everything going for it – health, stamina, fine temperament and outstanding show quality.

Abyssinian cats may be 'normal' in colour and are known as 'ruddy' in America, or they may be red. Both have the same type and conformation and differ only in colour, the former being marked with ticked hairs, rather like a wild rabbit, and the latter being a beautiful golden red. The latter are known as 'sorrel' in America, and this really is an excellent description of the true colour. These cats are of moderate foreign type, ears, head length, body and tail not being as extreme as those of the Siamese. White and tabby markings are considered bad faults in these varieties, but are very hard to eradicate, and an Abyssinian without a light chin is hard to find.

Burmese cats come in many colours. Some recognized in Britain are not recognized in America, but all possible colour permutations are, at present, being bred in both countries. From the original Burmese, known as the Brown Burmese in Britain and the Sable in America, natural dilution produced the Blue variety. Later, the recessive Chocolate colour turned up and from inter-mating cats carrying both blue and chocolate genes, the elusive silvery Lilac Burmese arrived. Red colouring was introduced in scientifically designed breeding programmes, and the full spectrum of sex-linked Red Burmese cats is now available, though rare. Red, Cream, Tortie, Chocolate-cream, Blue-cream and Lilac-cream have now been added to the British lists, although many of the varieties will not be eligible for championships for some years.

Havana cats are densely brown and gleam in the sunshine like fresh-dropped horsechestnuts. They are mischievous, and extremely intelligent, quieter than Siamese, but with the same dog-like devotion to their

owners. Extreme foreign type is called for in this breed, all features being long and lithe, the head very long and wedge-shaped, topped with large, wide-set ears. The expressive, almond eyes must also be wide-set, and of a definite clear green shade. Havanas do not like to be alone, and should never be kept unless in pairs or with a dog or human as a constant companion.

It is possible that the rex gene – that is, the one that causes the hair of a cat to be curled – turned up many times in the past, but it was not until 1950 that a curly coated kitten was noticed in a litter born to a farm cat in Cornwall, and a new breed was conceived. Ten years later, another curly kitten was discovered in Devon, and it was assumed that the rex gene was identical. Breeding tests proved this theory to be wrong, however, and we now have two quite separate types of rex cat, both curly coated, but otherwise quite distinct from each

other, and known as the Cornish Rex and the Devon Rex. While both breeds are of foreign type, subtle differences in bone structure and expression ensure that it is a simple task to distinguish between them, even for the novice.

Russian Blue cats are purported to have been brought from Archangel to Britain in the nineteenth century, but as the blue colour is merely due to the Maltese factor, a simple dilution of black, blue cats have been known for centuries. Whatever their beginnings, the Russian Blue cats are charming, quiet-voiced creatures of immaculate habits, and are determined, devoted pets. Of moderate foreign type, the Russian's ears are rather upright on the head, and the eyes are oval and of a clear, definite green. The coat is unique in this variety, being short, close and lustrous, like sealskin to the touch, and of a decided slate-blue colour emitting a silvery sheen as it catches the light.

The latest additions to the ranks of the foreign shorthaireds are the Foreign Lilac and the Foreign White. Both are extreme in type, looking like the Siamese from which they were derived. The Lilac has a coat of a beautiful silvery shade, rather like that of lavender bushes seen on a sunny day, with pads of pale pink and almond-shaped eyes of a deep clear green. The White is identical for type, with a pure-white coat and deep sapphire-blue eyes. Both varieties are similar in character, the Lilac being rather quieter than the White, and both make excellent pets for the flat or apartment, being quite content to live a confined life, so long as they have plenty of loving companionship.

Foreign shorthaireds are easy to breed, having large, even litters twice a year, seemingly without complications, and prove to be exceptional parents. The kittens are usually very forward and open their eyes at three to five days. They toddle early and may be out of the maternity box and tasting their mother's food at four weeks of age. Despite this, they are generally much smaller than longhaired or British shorthaired kittens of identical age, and often suffer teething setbacks, so should never go to new homes until at least twelve weeks old. Great escapologists, foreign queens have to be carefully confined during their very vocal periods of oestrus, and if not kept for breeding, should be neutered at about six months of age.

Red Abyssinian cats appeared spontaneously in litters as long ago as 1880, but it was many years before they were pioneered as a separate variety and were finally granted an official breed number in 1963 in Britain.

Far left
Foreign White cats are Siamese in white overcoats, for they are bred from this variety by the introduction of the dominant white gene which masks the points colour. Extremely foreign in type, the Whites are long, lithe and elegant, and have incredibly blue eye-colour.

Above
Blue Burmese first appeared in litters in the late 1950s as a simple dilution of the 'black' gene which produces the Brown Burmese. The coat colour in this variety is a lovely antique-silver tone, and must be sound and free from tabby markings and white hairs. The eyes of yellowish green set this off to perfection.

Left
Cornish Rex are a well-established breed on both sides of the Atlantic, and in America, success has been found in crossing the Cornish Rex, as shown here, with a German strain which appears to be genetically compatible. The Cornish Rex is bred for foreign type and should have a medium wedge head with a flat skull.

Above
This devoted Abyssinian mother cat is of the 'normal' variety, known in America as the Ruddy Abyssinian. She is particularly good, having no tabby markings or bars, but an evenly ticked coat of ruddy brown, the darker spine line being continued down the length of the tail.

Left
Most Abyssinian queens are good mothers, allowing their kittens to nurse, and bringing them food long after they are independent of her. They are very quiet when in oestrus, and become mismated unless great care is taken and the queen carefully confined.

Right
The eye-colour on this Blue Burmese kitten is remarkably good, for although the breed standard calls for yellowish eyes, many otherwise good examples are seen with definite green eyes, and this is considered a serious fault because it is so difficult to eradicate.

Right
Abyssinian kittens are born with very dark coats and often have dusky marks on their stomachs and bars on their front legs. Gradually the markings clear and the ticking begins to develop at about five weeks of age.

Below
This Havana kitten is British bred as can be seen by the Siamese type head and body. In America, the breed in known as the Havana Brown, and the standard is completely different, the cats having a unique 'puppy-dog' face. British Havana cats are now very popular and are often in the top awards at major cat shows.

Far right
Burmese kittens are born much paler than their finished adult coat colour will be, and these twins look most promising despite the fact that they are so sleepy. At ten weeks of age their domed skulls and medium wedge heads indicate that the correct head shape will develop when they become adults.

Far left
Recently, it was found that coats in some strains of rex were getting a little short of curl, and breeders have been working hard to rectify this with the excellent results that can be seen in this picture, for this beautiful cat is covered with a thick coat of tightly waved fur.

Left
Devon Rex cats are all descended from 'Kirlee', a kitten born to a stray tortie and white cat in 1960, in the county of Devon. These cats are bred in all coat colours, and have a wedge head with low-set ears, full cheeks and a quaint 'pixie' look.

Below
Rex kittens like these are hardy and full of fun. Despite their unusual coat structure, they do not seem to feel the cold unduly, and will romp in the garden on the coldest of days, but should not be allowed to get chilled.

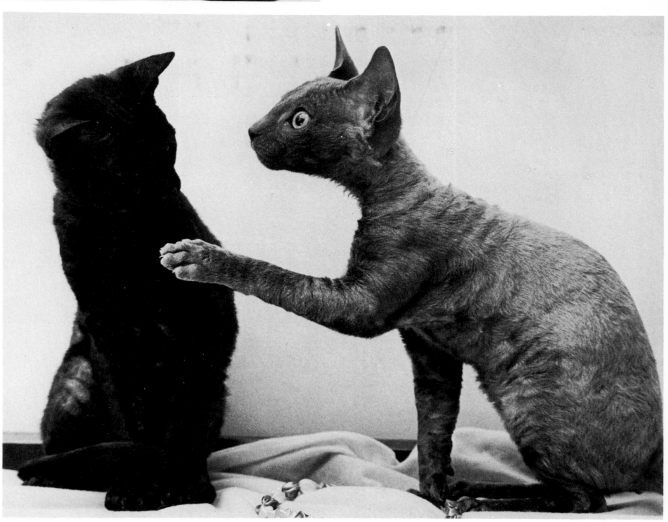

Top
The Russian Blue has a double coat which feels like
sealskin and emits a silvery sheen. Quiet-voiced and with
a very pleasant character, this cat makes the most
delightful pet and is particularly good with small
children.

Above
Red Burmese are the result of careful crossbreeding
within a scientifically designed breeding programme to
introduce the sex-linked red factor into the Burmese
breed. This young cat is a very good specimen having
a clear coat and really remarkable eye-colour.

Right
The Foreign Lilac is one of the newer breeds and is
known as the Oriental Lavender in America and as the
Lavendel in Europe. Bred carefully from selected
Siamese and Havana parents, the Lilac combines the
finest qualities of both, and is a uniquely beautiful, gentle
cat.

Above
The noble Russian Blue male in this picture is typical of his breed. Quiet and dignified, the males can be allowed access to their queens even when they are nursing litters, but are very aggressive with other male cats, ferociously defending their territory against intruders.

Right
Blue-cream Burmese are very unusual-looking cats, having the typical body shape of the Brown Burmese and the gentle pastel coat colour of the British Blue-cream. In the Burmese variety, the colours have an even more muted and slightly silvered effect, producing a cat of ethereal charm.

Above
The desired coat, free from all markings and beautifully ticked, must make the owner of this Red Abyssinian kitten very proud indeed. She also has the correct medium length of head with the slightly heart-shaped effect aimed for by breeders of this variety, and the slight head markings will soon disappear.

Right
Abyssinian cats were once known as 'ticked', 'British ticks' and 'bunny' cats, due to the unusual appearance of their coats, which closely resemble those of wild rabbits, each hair being banded with two or three lines of black, producing the ticked effect, known as agouti by geneticists.

Siamese

The first Siamese cats were brought to Britain from Thailand, then known as Siam, in 1884, and were thought to have been Seal-pointed, although some were said to have been brown, with yellow eyes. At the first British cat shows, several of these dark-pointed, blue-eyed creatures were exhibited and intrigued all who saw them. Since then, Siamese cats have prospered to become the most popular of all pedigreed cats throughout the world.

The early Siamese were delicate, and many died before maturity. Only the strongest survived the effects of being kept in hot-house conditions, and fed on brown bread and milk, to form the basis of the variety of Siamese that we now know. The early breeders learned by trial and error that the then rare breed needed plenty of meat, immunity to disease, and fresh air and exercise, in order to procreate, and it is thanks to their perseverance and perception that the Siamese has progressed to its present elevated status.

Siamese cats have long, svelte bodies and slim legs, the hind legs being longer than the forelegs, and long, whipped tails. The long, straight-profiled head is carried proudly on a long, elegant neck, and the large ears are wide at the base and widely set, forming a perfect triangle with the head. The beautiful, deep-blue eyes must be oriental in shape and widely set, following the line of the wedge head.

From the original Siamese Seal-pointed cats, three other colours have naturally emerged and the other recognized colours were the result of man's intervention in the scheme of things. Whatever the colour of the points, however, all Siamese cats must conform to the same standard for type and conformation, and all must have blue eye-colour. The points of the Siamese are the mask or face, the ears, tail and legs including the paws. In Seal-pointed, the points are a very dark seal-brown, in fact they appear almost black unless viewed in bright sunlight when the brownish tones may be seen.

Blue-pointed Siamese arrived spontaneously, due to the Maltese factor previously mentioned which diluted black to blue, and Chocolate-pointed Siamese also occurred when the simple recessive gene which inhibits dense colour came into being. When cats carrying both blue and chocolate factors mated, the Lilac-pointed Siamese was born. Although not recognized for what it was for some years, the recurrence of these ethereal, pastel-pointed Siamese eventually became noticed and it was given its recognition as a separate variety.

By introducing the sex-linked red factor into a strain of Siamese and then following up with several years of careful backcrossing, eventually Red-pointed Siamese of good type were produced. They and their closely allied Tortie-pointed female counterparts were given breed and championship status in several countries. Dilute red-pointed, known as Cream-pointed Siamese, and their female equivalents, the Chocolate-cream, Blue-cream and Lilac-cream Pointed females, also known as dilute Tortie-points, still await full status although they do have special classes at cat shows.

Tabby-pointed Siamese were also man-made, by the careful introduction of the tabby gene, and selective breeding programmes carried on. These cats are equal to Seal-points in type today, and may be had in Seal Tabby, Blue Tabby, Chocolate Tabby or Lilac Tabby, plus, of course, the Tortie Tabby, although this is not accepted in championship classes. Since their introduction in 1960, great interest has been shown in the variety and they became fully accepted in Britain in 1966. Many fine examples were exported to America, where they are known as Lynx-points in some associations and as Colorpoints in others.

Siamese cats should never be kept if they have to be left alone for long periods, for then they may pine. Two or more foreign cats may be kept together, or the Siamese may have a dog as a constant companion. These cats stay young forever, and always need a supply of toys and playthings – old boxes, cotton reels, stuffed mice and paper bags – to keep them amused. They can be great claw-stroppers and, if kept fully confined to the house for safety, will need a scratch-post, and be trained to use it instead of the furniture.

Highly intelligent, it is possible to train a pet Siamese to have perfect house manners, and to travel happily in the car or to take country walks. If kept free from draughts and vaccinated, the Siamese life-span is about fourteen years, and if given love and good food as well as daily handgrooming from head to tail, these will be fourteen full and unforgettable years. Neutered Siamese make perfect pets, always better in pairs in case they need boarding out or leaving for any length of time. Entire females may also be kept indoors, but will come into heat regularly if not mated, and are extremely vocal. Entire males can only be kept for stud purposes and must be carefully and correctly housed out of doors. Being extremely virile, their unpleasant spraying habits make them impossible as housepets.

Right
This beautiful, young Chocolate-pointed Siamese is using her claws to help her climb the tree. If kept indoors, these cats will damage the furniture with their claws if not provided with a scratch-post.

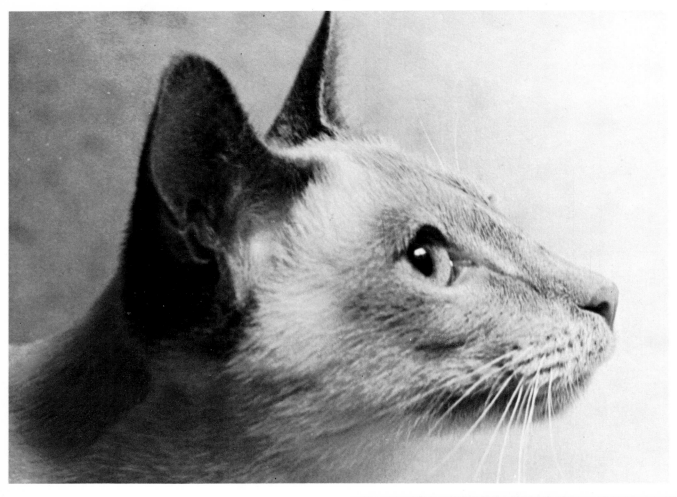

Above
Although the early Lilac-pointed Siamese tended to be rather cobby in build with heavy bone structure and rather short noses, careful breeding eventually produced superb specimens like this, with straight profiles and large, well-set ears.

Above right
The Seal-pointed, once known as the Royal Cat of Siam, is the original variety of Siamese cat. The pale cream body shades to a warm fawn on the flanks, and the face, tail, ears, legs and paws, known as the 'points', are a very dark seal-brown.

Right
At two weeks of age, the only stripes apparent on a Tabby-pointed Siamese kitten are those on the tail. 'Thumbprints' appear next on the backs of the ears, and a few days later, faint stripes are visible on the legs and cheeks.

Left
When buying a young Siamese which you hope will be your pet for many happy years, choose one that is lively, with an alert and intelligent expression; bright, clear, blue eyes; clean ears; and a soft, close-lying coat, free of pests.

Below
Chocolate-pointed Siamese are the most difficult to breed to standard, but this kitten is exceptionally good, having the desired ivory coat colour, and matching points of a rich chocolate shade, set off by decidedly blue eyes.

Right
No two Tortoiseshell-pointed Siamese are ever exactly alike, and this is the charm they hold for many fanciers. The desired blaze often gives a most bizarre expression, bisecting the long head between the fathomless blue eyes. Some cats of this variety present entirely different aspects when viewed from different sides.

Far left
The Red-pointed Siamese is an example of a man-made variety, and the original crosses were made between pure-bred Seal-points and red 'alley' cats. Many careful backcrosses to Siamese were made producing the near-perfect specimens of today, like this magnificent male.

Above
Lilac-pointed Siamese have magnolia-white body colour and points of a delicate dove-grey. They were developed by carefully planned matings, from Blue-pointed and Chocolate-pointed Siamese, and both parents needed to carry both genes for the elusive lilac colour to emerge in the kittens.

Left
Half-grown Siamese cats are full of fun and mischief and may get themselves lost while out at play. A soft leather collar specially made for cats, with an elastic insert for safety and an engraved name tag, may be worn by the young animal.

Above
Male cats of outstanding quality are often kept for stud purposes. They are comfortably housed in outdoor accommodation, and this excellent Blue-pointed Siamese, with his wedge head and oriental eyes, is quite content to sun himself in his wire-enclosed run.

Right
The points of the Red-pointed Siamese have been described in many ways, but the most apt would appear to be 'guinea-gold'. With his white coat and deep-blue eyes shining from the golden face, this variety is among the most striking of all foreign cats.

Far right above
Tabby-pointed Siamese come in all the normal Siamese colours, and this happy queen with her contented litter is a Blue Tabby-point. The body in this variety should be pale and the points striped and barred, with definite markings, like thumbprints on the backs of the ears.

Far right below
The type of this Lilac-point Siamese is perfect, the head narrowing in straight lines to a fine muzzle as called for in the standard, with the ears following the line of the wedge and superb oriental eyes of the correct colour. This is a cat that any Siamese fancier would love to own.

Right
This tiny Chocolate Tortie-pointed kitten is very typy, and a promising future brood queen, for if mated to a Cream-pointed Siamese or a Red-point carrying dilute genes, she could produce elusive Cream-pointed kittens of both sexes in her litter.

Below
Few sights can be more appealing than a sound and even litter of Siamese kittens. It would be hard to choose between these twelve-week-old Seal-points, with their sooty, intelligent faces, looking as alike as peas in a pod.

Far right
When a Seal-, Chocolate-, Blue- or Lilac-pointed female is mated to a Red-pointed male, the male kittens in the resulting litter have points to match those of the mother, while the female kittens have tortoiseshell points, in which the red from the sire is mingled with the colour of the dam's points. This is a Chocolate Tortie-pointed Siamese.

Left
A young and very beautiful Seal-pointed Siamese cat, showing an excellent length of head; a firm chin; large, well-set ears, wide at the base; good, dense seal-brown points; and superb, sapphire-blue eye-colour.

Above
This elegant Blue-pointed Siamese is proudly nursing her even, healthy litter. In this variety, the coat should be as white as possible, shading gradually into blue on the back and flanks, and even, slate-blue points.

Right
Young Siamese kittens are very inquisitive and love to sit inside any object new to them. Born pure white, the points begin to develop at about ten days and gradually spread and deepen until the correct colour can be determined at about seven weeks of age, as in this Seal-pointed kitten.

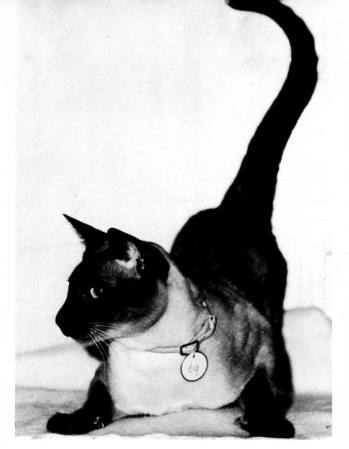

Far left
An excellent example of a Seal-pointed Siamese male cat in the peak of condition. His numbered tally, 'sixty-nine', shows that he was pictured while competing, and his raised tail indicates a calm and even temperament.

Left
At five weeks of age, few Siamese kittens can be expected to show their full exhibition potential, but this typy little Seal-point, posed in his mother's trophy, has every indication of becoming a future champion and announces the fact in true Siamese fashion.

Left
Kittens of the same age usually get along well together, even if of such diverse varieties as the Siamese and Abyssinian litters shown sharing a basket. The Siamese kittens will gradually develop their dense points, while the darkly smudged Abyssinians will lighten and clear.

Above
Man's intervention in the Siamese scheme of things produced the Tabby-pointed Siamese, which may be in any Siamese points colouring. This Seal Tabby-pointed Siamese is an excellent example of this popular variety with the desired face markings and barred tail.

Semi-longhaireds

The semi-longhaired breeds known in Britain are the Birman, or Sacred Cat of Birma, and the cat imported from the Lake Van district of Turkey, and once known as the Swimming Cat of Turkey, the Turkish. Both have been very carefully bred since their importation and no outside breeds have been introduced into their programmes at any stage. Thus, both breeds have been kept 'pure' and as they are intermediate both in type and length of coat, we refer to them as the semi-longhaireds.

Due to the Himalayan factor, the Birman has a pale body and dark points, like the Colourpoint Persian and the Siamese. At present, the points can be seal or blue, but other colours will obviously appear some time in the future. The outstanding feature of this breed, however, is the presence of striking white paws on all four feet. On the forefeet the white is sharply defined, being cut off like the wrists of white gloves across the ankles. On the hind feet, the white areas come to points at the heels, rather like gauntlets.

A charming legend surrounds the unusual colouring of the Birman. Centuries ago, a temple was built by the Khmer people of Asia to worship a sapphire-eyed, golden goddess called Tsun-Kyan-Kse. Before the statue of the goddess, Mun-Ha, a fervent priest, sat in constant meditation, accompanied by his faithful white cat, Sinh. When raiders attacked and killed his master one night, Sinh sat guarding the body, his feet upon his dead master and his eyes gazing at the statue. As he stood there, his yellow eyes turned to the blue of those of the goddess, his white body changed to a golden hue and his legs turned to the brown of the earth, except for his paws, for where they remained in contact with Mun-Ha's body, they remained pure-white. The hundred temple cats also changed as had Sinh, and on the seventh day of his vigil, Sinh finally died, taking with him to paradise the soul of his beloved master. Since that day, whenever a sacred temple cat died, it was said to take with it the soul of a dead priest, to paradise.

At the beginning of this century the temple at Lao-Tsun was raided and the priests were aided by two westerners, whom they rewarded by presenting them with a pair of temple cats. Later, further pairs of Birman cats were sent to France and from these precarious beginnings the breed is at last starting to prosper. Imports into Britain were made in 1960, recognition was granted in 1966, and the breed is now well established.

Possessed of a wonderful temperament, the Birman is intelligent, loving and gentle. Its sweet nature makes it easy to handle and show, and because of the texture of the fine, semi-longhaired coat, needs much less grooming than the Persian cats. Nevertheless, it should receive a daily comb-through to keep the coat knot-free. Less extreme in type than the regular Persians, the Birman has a round head with full cheeks, and a medium-length nose. The round eyes should be deep-blue in the Seal-pointed variety and china-blue in the Blue-pointed, and the wide-set ears should not be as tiny as those of the Persians. Great importance is paid by judges to the white gloves and gauntlets, which must be according to the standard and in well-matched pairs.

Turkish cats have been domesticated in the Lake Van district of Turkey for centuries and are much loved and highly prized by their masters. Very intelligent and affectionate, their liking for playing and swimming in ponds and horse troughs gained them fame as 'swimming cats'. An English woman travelling in Turkey in 1955 was given a pair of these unusual cats, and becoming enamoured of their unique character and temperament, made further trips to and from Turkey, to increase breeding stock in Britain.

Now fully recognized in Britain and really well-established, this variety has been kept absolutely pure, and

is never outcrossed with any other breed. The cats are strong and adaptable and completely unique in type, and although longcoated, require very little grooming as they have no woolly undercoats to mat up. The Turkish cat is chalk-white in colour and has brilliant auburn markings on the head, with a white blaze. The head is a medium-length wedge, topped by large and upright ears, well-feathered on the outside and a delicate, shell-pink inside. The round, light-amber eyes have pink-skinned rims. Perhaps the most striking feature of all, however, is the magnificent full brush, which is auburn with darker auburn rings.

Sturdy and renowned for their stamina, Turkish cats thrive on plenty of fresh air and exercise and a good, balanced diet which includes a proportion of fresh, raw meat. They mate up fairly easily, although queens may be a little shy upon introduction to a male in strange surroundings, and have their kittens easily, usually three or four. They are possessive mothers and do not like outside interference or visitors admiring their babies, before weaning.

This young Birman cat has attained his true colouring, with the soft, pale coat in sharp contrast to the seal-brown points. His four, immaculate, white feet are also in evidence, and his eye-colour, even at this age, seems a good blue.

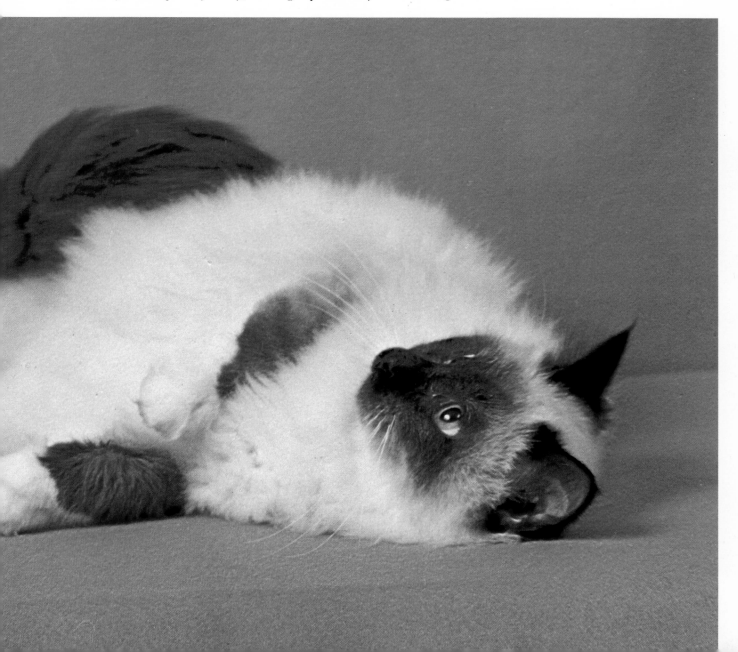

In this series of pictures a delightful little Turkish kitten aged about four or five weeks was placed on a tree trunk to have her portrait made. At first (*above left*) she was quite happy and interested in all that was going on around her then (*below left*) panic set in and she began to call for help. Her watchful mother soon answered her call (*above*) and cast a baleful eye at the photographer until (*opposite*) the kitten was safely restored to her at ground level, and all traces of human handling carefully removed.

Left
Turkish cats prefer to be out and about rather than being confined to quarters, and their unusual colouring is set off to advantage by a fresh green lawn. These cats are very hardy, coming from a district which often has snow for half of each year.

Above
It is difficult to believe that this tiny little auburn and white scrap will turn out to be a silky, longcoated Turkish cat. This breed has two, three or four kittens in each litter, and the kittens are small but sturdy.

Left
This glorious Blue-pointed Birman queen proudly
displays her two very typy babies, her benign expression
clearly demonstrating the wonderful temperament and
love for humans that these cats possess.

Above
A very fine and even litter of Birman kittens, three
Seal-pointed and two Blue-pointed, the colour on the
points developing well and the paws clearly marked with
the correct amount of white. Even at this tender age
the coat length is good and this is a very promising
litter.

These young Seal-pointed Birman kittens, relaxed but interested in all that is going on around them, typify the Birman character. Easy to rear and naturally house-trained, the kittens of this variety are rare and it is sometimes necessary to book well ahead.

Left
These Birman twins are Seal-pointed and follow the
American and Canadian standard which clearly defines
the Birman head shape as strong, broad and rounded,
and the nose, Roman in shape, medium in length with
the nostrils set low.

Above
The majestic, male Birman has a long, silky coat, slightly
curled on the belly, his body is slightly longer than the
regular Persian body, and so is the bushy tail. The
full-cheeked, round head is slightly flattened above the
eyes, and he should sport a good ruff as does the one
in our picture.

American breeds and new breeds

Several breeds which are in the developmental stages in Britain are fully recognized in America, and there are some breeds which are well-established in America for which there are no immediate plans in Britain. Being so diverse and interesting, they deserve a place in this book, their evocative names firing the imagination: Cameo, Peke-face, Korat, Sphynx and others.

The Cameo cat is a Persian of regular type, and is produced by adding silver and red genes to any copper-eyed Persian, such as Tortoiseshell to Smoke. The resulting kittens, used as a foundation stock, are then bred down the generations, and eventually Cameo Persians are born, correct for type and colour. Basically a red cat with a silver undercoat, the Cameo has six permutations of colour. Firstly the 'red' can be full red or diluted to cream, although in America only red is allowed. In each of these colours, three tones can arise: first the Shell Cameo, with light red or cream tipping; slightly darker is the Shaded Cameo; and thirdly the Smoke Cameo, seemingly red all over, although blowing into the coat reveals the white undercoat.

The Shaded Silver is really just a heavily marked Chinchilla cat and is extremely beautiful. A Persian in all points, the white coat is heavily ticked with black, giving a sparkling effect. A shorthaired variety, called the Exotic Chinchilla, is being bred in America and is caused by the same gene, but is not yet apparent in British cat shows.

A spontaneous longhaired mutation is said to be the cause of the appearance of the Balinese, which is a Siamese in features except that it has a semi-longhaired coat and a very full brush. Type is as for Siamese, with a straight profile; large, pointed ears; and almond-shaped, vivid-blue eyes. Recognized in America, a few imports have been made into Britain where breeding programmes have been formulated.

Peke-face Persians first appeared in the early 1930s and are only recognized in America, where it it is still a rare breed. Only bred in red and red-tabby, the peke-faced feature is the result of the naturally heavy folds found in the faces of the early Red Self and Red Tabby Persians, which were selected for and developed into this breed. The face of this variety should resemble that of a Pekingese dog, with a short, depressed or indented nose and a decidedly wrinkled muzzle. The very large, round eyes are set wide apart, prominent and brilliant, copper in colour.

Korat cats were considered to be the good-luck charms of the Thai people, and a few specimens were imported into America in the 1930s from which they have been carefully developed as a pure breed. A few British breeders have imported Korat cats and are working to gain recognition for them. The Korat is a self-coloured,

blue shorthair of medium foreign type, and has large, green-gold eyes offsetting the lovely silvery sheen of the coat. Unlike the Russian Blue, the Korat has a single coat of short to medium-length glossy hair, which breaks over the spine in movement.

A hairless male kitten was born to an ordinary house-cat in 1966, in Ontario, Canada, and started a breeding programme for the development of the Sphynx, or Canadian Hairless Cat. A very fine down is apparent on

the paws, up to the waist and ankle, and on the tail-tip, and other down is present on the points of the head. All colours are acceptable and the eyes are golden. This breed is recognized by some American associations, but is not bred in Britain.

Also absent from the British show scene is the Japanese Bobtail, known for centuries in Japan and depicted in many paintings and scrolls. Clannish in nature, the Bobtails have tails only two or three inches long although they have the correct number of vertebrae. The coat pattern is tricoloured in black, red and white, and type is intermediate between British and foreign.

Another mutation occurred among farm cats in America in 1966 when a wire-haired kitten was discovered in an otherwise normal litter. Being a dominant gene, great strides have been possible in developing this feature, and the cats are most attractive, being purely domestic in appearance, intermediate in type, the only difference being in the coat which is medium in length, coarse, stiff and wiry.

Egyptian Mau cats in America originated from two cats imported from Cairo in 1950, and a pure line has been attempted from the original pair. The standard allows for Bronze which is equivalent to the Brown Tabby in British shorthair coloration, or Silver which equals the Silver Tabby or Spottie. They are of medium foreign type and the desired pattern is clear spotting. Egyptian Mau cats are also bred in Britain, but are not recognized for championship status. They have been carefully bred from Siamese in an attempt to re-create the ancient Egyptian cat as seen in the bronzes, and the British standard requires the chocolate gene to be much in evidence giving bronze spotting on a warm chestnut background, plus a clearly defined 'scarab' beetle mark between the ears.

It is not possible to cover all the experimental breeding programmes in this book, but some varieties being developed in Britain and America deserve a mention. The most striking at present is the Foreign Black, known as the Oriental Black in America and as the Ebony in Europe. This cat has been so carefully bred that its type is that desired for the perfect Siamese. The coat colour is a dense, sound glossy black, with no trace of white hairs and the oriental eyes are a vivid green.

Abyssinian cats are also being bred in new colours – cream, blue and lilac, plus an exotic silver shade which is most attractive. With the distinctive Abyssinian heart-shaped face and lynx-like ears, the new varieties within this breed should rapidly gain in popularity.

Pastel cats are the result of adding the silver gene to the existing self-coloured foreign breeds, and most attractively tinted experimental litters have been bred in Britain. The kittens look, at first glance, like their self-coloured counterparts but gradually the undercoat develops so that it is always apparent in the adult. This underneath colour is white or silver, giving a beautiful shot-silk effect to the adult cat.

Thought to have originated from crosses between Persian cats brought home by ancient seafarers, and local, lynx-like wildcats, the Maine Coon is a well-loved breed. It is renowned for its health and delightful disposition, and may be of any recognized colour.

Left
Korats live happily in family 'prides', the male taking delight in helping with the raising of his kittens. These cats do not flourish in large, cattery conditions, and are best kept in small, family units in the house.

Above
The ethereal Shell Cameo may appear white from a distance but on closer inspection, each long, silky, white hair is seen to be tipped with pale red. The eyes are copper in colour and because of the care given to the selection of stock for the formation of the breed, these cats are very healthy.

Below
The rare and exotic Egyptian Mau has markings which closely resemble those of cats depicted on the papyrus records of ancient Egypt.

Right
The Shaded Silver is a heavily tipped Chinchilla and is a very beautiful cat indeed, the tipping producing more of a pewter shade than the silver effect caused by the light black tipping in the Chinchilla. Otherwise both breeds are very alike and kittens of both types appear in the same litter.

Below right
Healthy, happy carefree cats, the Balinese combine the best qualities of the Siamese with the beauty of a full, but easy-to-maintain, flowing coat.

Above
Shaded Silver cats may be rare and beautiful, but are easy to care for, needing a quick comb-through each day to prevent the tangling of the long, silky coat, and a powdering perhaps once a week, when the teeth and ears may be checked also.

Right
Balinese is the name given to the mutation which occurred in America in 1954, when some kittens in a litter of pure-bred Siamese ancestry, developed long, silky coats.

Left
Quiet and gentle, the Korat cat, or Si-Sawat as it is known in Thailand, has been bred true for many generations, and thus has retained its natural form to a great extent. Robust and adaptable, the Korat has been recognized in America for some years and it was recently introduced to Britain.

Below
Lightly ticked with palest cream, the Shell Cameo has a pure white undercoat, which produces the overall, desired, pale-pink, sparkling effect. Amber, orange or copper eyes, rimmed with deep rose-pink add to the stunning appearance of this systematically produced variety.

Right
In America, the Egyptian Mau is descended from two spotted cats imported from North Africa in 1953, while in England the variety has been scientifically reproduced by planned breeding programmes.

Left
This Havana queen, known to carry the blue factor,
was mated with a Chocolate Tabby-pointed Siamese
hoping to found the bases of some new colour strains.
Her interesting litter contained two Foreign Lilac kittens,
founders of the variety in Britain; a Lilac and a Bronze
Egyptian Mau; an Havana, later to be a famous
champion; and one, lone Chocolate-pointed Siamese.

Above
The foreign kittens from the Havana's litter, left to right:
Solitaire Archil, Foreign Lilac male; Solitaire Aloha,
Havana female; Solitaire Amethyst, Foreign Lilac
female; Solitaire Amulette, Bronze Mau female; Solitaire
Attaboy, Lilac Mau male.

Non-pedigreed cats

Since the hungry cat first made his tentative approach to man's camp-fire, a tolerant and sometimes affectionate relationship has sprung up, cat and man accompanying each other through the pages of history. No home seems complete without a cat, whether it be a pampered Persian or a homely little ex-stray.

All cats need the same essential care – a good, well-balanced diet; a warm bed; careful attention to vaccination programmes, reproduction and eradication of parasites: plus a good two-way relationship between cat and human, so that both may benefit from the sharing of the fireside.

Non-pedigree cats make superb pets so long as they have been carefully handled from kittenhood, for it is in the important imprinting time from about five weeks of age that the character of the cat is largely formed. Kittens in the nest subjected to slightly stressful conditions, being examined and handled for a few moments each day, develop their full brain potential, and when handled and played with from seven or eight weeks onwards, become very loving in nature and human-orientated.

Thus it is very difficult, though not wholly impossible, to tame wild, farm or feral kittens, for although they may become house cats, they always seem to have an irrational streak in them, and are difficult with strangers and almost impossible to board out during the holidays. Some pedigree cats are like this also, and it is interesting to trace back their past record which usually reveals that their breeder was a firm believer in not 'interfering' with the upbringing of the kittens, and having them shut well away from the everyday running of the house.

House cats come in every shape, size and colour imaginable and most are shorthaired, although some semi-longhaired pet cats are seen. Areas of rural countryside build up indigenous cat populations and so it is common to find villages wherein most cats are blue and white, or perhaps tortoiseshell. In some areas where long ago a Siamese male was allowed to wander, the genes have asserted themselves and Siamese patterned cats of all sorts of shapes, some fluffy, even some tailless, may be found.

More and more people are keeping cats confined to the house these days, mainly to keep their pets safe from the increasingly heavy traffic, and from cat thieves who sell cats to laboratories, or for their skins. Being so fastidious in their habits, cats can be happily kept indoors, but must be provided with a toilet tray, changed daily, a scratching post, and a pot of grass to chew.

When choosing a non-pedigree kitten, always try to see the whole litter and notice whether the mother is docile or nervous, and if she appears to be in good health. She may be very thin, for a good mother turns most of her food intake into milk while lactating, but her eyes should be bright and clear with no sign of discharge and there should be no unpleasant odour about her, the kittens or the nest.

The kittens should be alert and playful, with clear, bright eyes and the inside of the ears should be clean and pink with no gritty discharge which could be a symptom of canker. The nose should be dry, and the tail end free from staining which could indicate diarrhoea. It is unlikely that the owner of a non-pedigree queen will have gone to the expense of having the kittens inoculated against feline infectious enteritis, and may

well be trying to find new homes for them before they have reached the required age for the injection. Having first made sure that the kitten you have chosen is able to lap and eat solids, and therefore can be independent of its mother, take him in a warmly lined carrier to the veterinary surgeon for a thorough examination, and to book his inoculation at a suitable date.

On arrival home, make sure that there are no hidden hazards, such as chimneys to hide up, live flex to chew on, things to fall down from, and tiny spaces to crawl into. Confine the kitten to an area to which he can become accustomed and where he can easily find his toilet tray. Give him a warm and secluded bed and some food and water, and let him learn his way about your home from this safe base.

This is one of the many times that you will gain if you have been really sensible and acquired two kittens instead of one. Two kittens, by some magical mathematical process known only to themselves, manage to provide much more than twice the fun and enjoyment gained from one kitten. At all stressful times – being left alone, being left at the kennels, recovering from a minor operation and especially in changing homes – cats cope much better if they are in pairs raised from kittenhood together. Any boarding cattery proprietors will confirm that their favourite inmates are pairs of cats from the same home, for they do not pine, they eat all their meals and go home looking even better than when they arrived. If finances or space preclude you from having more than one cat, then you must take the place of the missing feline by providing many and varied toys and games and setting aside a daily play hour, in which you take turns at being the hunter and the hunted, the stalker and the prey.

Pet cats should be vaccinated or inoculated against disease at three months, and may need yearly or two-yearly boosters depending upon the vaccine used. Twice-yearly treatment against infestation with roundworms is advisable also and this is a good time to get your veterinary surgeon to check on your pet's teeth, claws and ears, which are renowned troublespots. Neutering can be carried out at any age on both male and female cats, but each veterinary surgeon has his own favourite age to operate on kittens so take his advice. Many people think it is kinder to let the female cat have just one litter of kittens before she is spayed, but this is very wrong, for it is a relatively simple operation when performed on a young female, and much more serious after the birth of a litter.

Cat shows are held for non-pedigree cats, the most famous of all being run by the National Cat Club at Olympia, London, each winter. Here, some five hundred cats of all shapes and sizes have one quarter of the massive show hall for their own special section, and compete for the coveted rosettes and trophies and maybe the chance to appear on television. People from all walks of life, from dukes to dustmen, exhibit their cats at the 'National', all having the same common bond, love and admiration for that most gracious of all creatures, the cat.

Young, growing animals may need as many as four, well-balanced feeds to promote good health.

Left
The tail-up greeting is the cat's way of politely waiting for his morning milk, and is often a prelude to leg-rubbing, another form of affectionate greeting in the cat, quite as expressive as speech.

Below
Even a torn-eared tom likes to find a warm and comfortable spot for his afternoon's siesta and what could be better than the still-hot bonnet of a recently parked car?

Right
Adult, neutered pets require only one main meal per day, with, maybe, a small snack in the mornings.

Below right
It is quite a good idea to hang a bell around the neck of any cat likely to catch precious garden birds, but this tiny kitten does not really look to be much of a menace yet.

Left
It is difficult to believe that these two tubby tabbies were once sad little strays in the streets of London. Good food and tender loving care has transformed them into this delightful pair of healthy pets.

Below
A kitten's first steps in the great world of the outdoors are carefully watched over by its protective mother, who teaches the first rudimentary steps in stalking and hunting, and gradually encourages the youngster to be independent.

Right
This pet longhair is in wonderful condition, and is very attractive with bright, clear, green eyes shining out of a coal-black face.

Left

All kittens love to play. Their behaviour at this time prepares them for stalking, hunting and mating in later life, and is thus a vital part of their development. It has been proved that kittens encouraged to play a great deal, develop more brain cells than those raised in confinement.

Below left

Most communities have a stray-cat problem, and some of these are solved by groups of cat-lovers who get together and raise cash to set up a sanctuary such as this. Stray cats are rescued, nursed to health and then found suitable homes.

Above

All cats love to climb and some prove to be much better at it than others. This intrepid tabby is venturing out on to branches too slender to take his weight, but is testing carefully with the forepaws before moving forward, the claws unsheathed for a better grip.

Above right

These two felines gained fame as kittens when they crossed the Atlantic Ocean in a perilous three-month voyage on board a small raft. As the picture shows, they were none the worse for their adventures.

Right

All kittens love to get into small, dark spaces and this little blue and white pet shorthair is no exception. He thought the shopping bag ideal for napping, but the sounds of mealtime roused him from his slumbers, and he drowsily emerges.

Left
Black and White cats are very common among house
pets, and rarely are two identically marked, which adds
to their charm. In pet-cat shows, they are often among
the top winners if presented in sparkling condition and
with snow-white paws and bib.

Above
All sorts of cats arrive in need of care and rehabilitation
at the many sanctuaries run by animal welfare societies
throughout the world. Many are past recovery, but some,
as this beautiful, lynx-like longhair, return to full health,
and await kind, new homes.

Right
This is a sign of a contented cat. After a satisfying and
tasty meal, most cats thoroughly remove every scrap
of food from their lips with a long, flexible tongue, before
using a well-licked paw to wash the rest of the face.

Above left
It is easy to see that this wonderfully marked, black
and white longhair is someone's much-loved pet, for she
is in glowing health and her shining coat is offset by
an immaculate white bib and blaze.

Left
Cats sometimes have long hair growing between the toes
and this must be watched carefully, as small stones, twigs,
dried mud or even ice may mat the hair together causing
great pain if left unattended. Older cats, in particular,
may find it difficult to clean long hair in this region.

Above
This sweet little tabby-and-white kitten, too small to
be an adept hunter, nevertheless is cute enough to climb
up the back of the chair to take a closer look at the
photographer's gadgets.

Above
Although this cat is obviously answering back to his mistress, and not snarling, it enables us to take a good look at his well-designed teeth, made for gripping prey and biting and tearing meat. Domestic cats suffer from tooth decay unless fed a carefully chosen diet.

Left
Newcomers, even if friendly neighbours, are treated with cautious indifference and given a wide berth.